W0016606

Looking into the Heart of Light

University of Central Florida
Contemporary Poetry Series

George Bogin, *In a Surf of Strangers*
Van K. Brock, *The Hard Essential Landscape*
Rebecca McClanahan Devet, *Mother Tongue*
Gerald Duff, *Calling Collect*
Malcolm Glass, *Bone Love*
Susan Hartman, *Dumb Show*
Lola Haskins, *Planting the Children*
William Hathaway, *Looking into the Heart of Light*
Roald Hoffmann, *The Metamict State*
Hannah Kahn, *Time, Wait*
Michael McFee, *Plain Air*
Richard Michelson, *Tap Dancing for the Relatives*
David Posner, *The Sandpipers*
Nicholas Rinaldi, *We Have Lost Our Fathers*
CarolAnn Russell, *The Red Envelope*
Robert Siegel, *In a Pig's Eye*
Edmund Skellings, *Face Value*
Edmund Skellings, *Heart Attacks*
Ron Smith, *Running Again in Hollywood Cemetery*
Don Stap, *Letter at the End of Winter*

Looking into the Heart of Light

Poems by

William Hathaway

University of Central Florida Press
Orlando

Copyright © 1988 by William Hathaway
All rights reserved
Printed in the U.S.A. on acid-free paper. ∞

৯৮

Library of Congress Cataloging-in-Publication Data

Hathaway, William, 1944–
    Looking into the Heart of Light : poems / by William
    Hathaway
        p. cm. — (University of Central Florida contem-
    porary poetry series)
        ISBN 0-8130-0901-4 (alk. paper) : $10.00
        I. Title.   II. Series.
    PS3558.A75L66   1988
    811'.54—dc19   88–19133
                                                              CIP

৯৮

University Presses of Florida is the central agency for
scholarly publishing of the State of Florida's university
system, producing books selected for publication by the fac-
ulty editorial committees of Florida's nine public univer-
sities: Florida A&M University Press (Tallahassee), Florida
Atlantic University Press (Boca Raton), Florida International
University Press (Miami), Florida State University Press
(Tallahassee), University of Central Florida Press (Orlando),
University of Florida Press (Gainesville), University of
North Florida Press (Jacksonville), University of South Flor-
ida Press (Tampa), University of West Florida Press (Pensa-
cola).

Orders for books published by all member presses should be
addressed to University Presses of Florida, 15 NW 15th
Street, Gainesville, FL 32603.

Acknowledgments

Some of these poems were originally published in:
The Antioch Review
St. Andrews Review
Quarterly West
Poet & Critic
Tar River Review
The Chariton Review
Poetry
North American Review
Colorado State Review
Cincinnati Poetry Review
NER/BLQ
Memphis State Review
New Letters
Pembroke Magazine
American Poetry Review
Salmagundi
Mid-American Review
Kansas Quarterly
Green Mountains Review .
Ecstatic Occasions, Expedient Forms, edited by David
    Lehman (New York: Macmillan, 1987)
*Contemporary American Poetry: Some Poets of the
    80's*, edited by Jack Myers and Roger Weingarten
    (Key West: Wampeter Press, 1986)

"But Faith, like a jackal, feeds among the tombs, and even from these dead doubts she gathers her most vital hope."
　　　—Herman Melville, *Moby Dick*

"Peccantem me quotidie et non poenitentem timor mortis conturbat me. Quia in inferno nulla est redemptio misere mei Deus et salva me."　—*Office of the Dead*

"I was neither
Living nor dead, and I knew nothing,
Looking into the heart of light, the silence.
Oed' und leer das Meer."
　　　—T. S. Eliot, "The Wasteland"

" 'On ne peut penser et ecrire qu'assis.' (C. G. Flaubert)—Now I have you nihilist! Assiduity is a *sin* against the holy spirit. Only ideas *won by walking* have any value."
　　　—Friedrich Nietzsche, "Maxims and
　　　　Arrows," no. 34, *Twilight of
　　　　the Idols*

Contents

December Eighth, 1
When I Consider, 3
Deer Season Again, 10
American Gogol, 13
Wan Hope, 15
Tremble, 18
This Tree, 20
Cayuga Heights Crows, 23
East Polk Street Park, 25
Spit, 28
Greyhound/Science Fiction, 30
December 18th, 1944, 33
Negative Incapability, 34
Idle Tears, 37
Impatience, 39
The Giants' Game, 41
Beholding Nothing, 43
Inflation, 44
Oh, Oh, 45
Peach Pit, 46
In Each Day, 48
At Susanne's School, 50
At the Jet Show, 51
Catfish Grumble, 53
The Jungle Gym, 56
The Tongue, 58
Kipling at Southsea, 60
The Popsicle Scepter, 63
Scallops in Garlic Sauce, 65
A New Laugh, 67

Salt Treatment, 69
Riding the Lions, 72
Biloxi Beach, 74
Vacationer, 76
He Couldn't Know, 78
The End of the World, 80
Paratactic Prayer, 82
Timor Mortis: Sermo, 84

About the author, 94

December Eighth

In the beginning was the Word
so they wrecked that right away.
Some always ask "Just *who* are *they?*"
nasaling a sneer on the pronouns—the ones
I mean. But we, us, got born from zero
with zero to make hours match dollars.
We call sit-down jobs they call careers
good luck and tap any laminated gleam
for hope. In office drowse we still moon
for that Word teetering on the mind's tip.
Yes, the sea murmured it ceaselessly
and it breathed warm on our moist skin ...
O loony us! Real luck, self-evidently,
gets made by bloody hands or sweaty heads.

But a hunch nags us that today
is somehow infamous. Just another workday:
we pick up papers, put them down in place.
All words get processed, quick-dried
and pressed to pages. In the names
of our true voices we send forth wet sounds
to squirm promiscuously in the wires.
We tuck receivers under our chins
to shuffle words with our hands
and we drone yeah-yeah-yeah often,
with even stress. Perhaps our secret minds
recollect those "Mischievous Mopheads,"
as they called them, who warbled
that triple affirmative on an upbeat.
Now they soap up for each new day's luck
singing "I love me yup-yup-yup"

to morning mirrors. And we don't sing
at all. We hum dusty snatches,
distant as voices in the wires.

If a dirge murmurs in the mind,
we might hear that forlorn pistol crack
crumpling the man-child singer
who teased us with his hope. The meek
didn't mob the court where the mad
judged the sanity of the mad.
We stopped singing and learned to hum,
stressless as a drone of Jap zeroes
swarming from the zero beyond the sea's
edge to bang our time to life.

They don't know we hum like bombs.
Secret as a hieroglyph, a Word
hums in our tongue roots. It squirms
in spraypaint curlicues on their trains
and buildings. Any day now,
like today, when the season's first Santa
jangles a cold street for a drink
while we sit at our jobs of work—
on just such a day as this, Infamy
could burst from behind a cloud
again. And we will shout our Word.

When I Consider

There's much light here and also music,
but it's not the light Milton meant
lamenting the divine economy. Oh Christ!
From brightest aisles, where silver baskets
glide past a glitter of goods—even here
I hear the whole world's choral whine ascend.
"Shaddup, you little shit!" The teenage harlot's
curse blasts her infant's bawl. In the air-
sucking lull of its shriek "Theme to *A Summer
Place*" whispers out of fluorescence. Here,
I must consider. Is this a moment for sermon:
Urizen? Remember, preach not yourself
as truth; imperfect yet you may only bear it.
For my heart has split in pity for her face,
scalded swollen with tears as saline hot
as any shed by Io—so ripple out
infinite circles of fear. But what's pity?
A soul-slasher for no cigar. And I, gone gray
not from lightbursts of epiphanic pain
but from gravity's matter-of-factual grind—
should I drop to the linoleum this box
of soap with its promise in bright red print
not to blight, too much, my septic
and thus our world and in the midst
of this radiant maze clasp her face close
into the cool dark of my jean jacket?
Then submit like Jesus to the long march
in irons and thorns past the check-out,
to the indifferent hand shoving my head
from sight under a languid twirl of light . . . ?

Considering—*cum sidus*—is my text.
And I do lament that Milton is impossible,
as he was storming blind in ecstatic joys
and profound grumps at his sermons' moments.
And yes, I confess I was a bad-old-boy
as a critic claimed, following Johnson's
first disobedience to the Master. My head
dusty-hot and overhassled, I tossed aside
the Norton and went abroad in search
of companions. But I've thumbed back again
and like that reviewer seen the miracle
of cells pop back from lysol in tile grout.
Even if your brain's a turnip so you just sit
and wait day after day in the dark, a slow,
steady drool, pink hands twitching on your lap
like baby possums dozing, watching a box
of flitting light and shadow while Mother
drinks beer in the kitchen with men
in canvas vests and orange plastic hats—
even then the skin's invisible creep over
your sores signals a magical salvation ...

Crap! All of us professor-poets have seen
snapshots in lit-prize magazines of our friends
breaking bread in the old Frost cabin
where a much-discussed wine seems to generate
its own stars in each poet's crystal globe.
We've also taken the *dopo pranzo* arms-on-shoulders
stroll out under sane New Hampshire's
galactic glare. You can't help but consider
how vulnerable is that small warmth between
the tummy and the heart, and what can be done
against the dark but pick up round pebbles
off the road to press in each others' palms.
Each clutching a holy stone so hard it seems
a fact that rocks whisper the sweetest sighs

4

a sound can make. Swept up in honeyed sorrow
to a *naiv und sentimentalisch* gush—O where
is there to look but down? Down to angry lights
from the trailer park in town where oafs
we call "America's pure products" stare goat-
eyed into squares of violence without a poem
in their hearts. The dead Pegasus Tennyson beat
to purple rot still gets its spare bones
clattered, dried meat whipped to dust ...
But does it still take one to know one?

For I've also stood around waiting
under the mild yoke of a professorship
to feel like Shelley on a third dip in
the punch. Even in my fiercest boyhood
atheism, devil-talking Jeff Nulle out of
the priesthood under streetlights home from
scoutmeetings, my rutabaga heart willed to
believe deep in its proprioceptive chug
that beyond all reason this time/space
Gloom-Shaboom is far-out there somewhere
englobed in Love's blinding radiance.
One fast snooze was Rev. Dodd's vacuous
promise and then a well-lit bliss. When he
died and the young geewhizzer for Jesus
strummed Kingston Trio during church, I turned
to Modern Art for good and never did go back.

Even earlier, I was sent on rainy Sundays
for the sake of science to museums or
the planetarium. Outside, a gray drizzle
in the park soaked bare tree trunks black
and the city howled and screeched like a zoo
full of creatures maddened from loneliness.
Inside, a man in a gray suit began to say
the words of science while over all an utter

5

darkness fell and around him bloomed a spot
of light. I listened only to an undulant drone
without sense. Rain muttering to the dark dirt,
urgent gusts of joy whispering down to soft
dirge—like I guessed blind poets consider voices.
By pressing and unplugging my ears at random
like bored boys do in church, I heard
distinct words—*dwarf, gas, eon*—resound
out of a watery void, as in a grand old invocation.
But if I forbore my childish game, this talk
was not a poem or sermon, but science—portentous
in the absolute light of fact. This witness
was not a *Sciet Omnia*, not one of our know-it-
all-shits of art & humanity who haul you out
past the woodpile to consider wildflowers
of the field, birds and foxes in dens, and oh,
my stars by naming them in latin, greek
and Algonquin—so much grist for poetical mills.
This man's matter-of-fact voice owned the words
those others rented, and oddly, more in Blakean sway
than Miltonic fustion. As he spoke, a music
groaned up from bass depths with human squeals
mingled in, like spooky cries over misty water.
One by one, and then in pyrotechnic clusters
stars blinked on in the dome, as if his voice
in rising sparked them. I'd pick one star
to keep as mine, my center, through it all
but somehow in the crescendo's shriek and glare
I'd always lose my star in the milky smear.

And so the universe on a Sunday began
with burst of fiery seeds and ended
like a bomb—blowing out and sucking in,
a terrible slow breathing in the dark.
When I quit my magic clowning with my ears,

his voice rose and lilted along in a usual
warble. And that's just our own universe,
he said, beyond this nothing extends another
and then ever more nothing that's even less
than space, which always seemed as nothing
as anything can get. Only the laugh at the end
of his lame little jokes cackled like a kid's
plastic pistol. Like a dull adult who turns
on the light to show us nothing's there,
he clearly saw without perceiving and heard
beyond understanding and stood without fear
in empty light. Outside on the darkening
street I pressed fingers on my eyelids
And stars burst to flame again! Inside!

I wondered if the blind see black darkness
or gray-white light of an empty screen.
Always, blind poets invoke a night where
stars, real or unseen, shine and I imagined
a burst of brilliant light at the end
of a long life's darkness. Then the nothing
we cannot imagine. Infinite waves from stars'
factual light, even stars far beyond
the billions our machines can own by name,
seemed less than dustmotes, or electrons
hissing out in an entropic fizzle in grains
of sand on the Red Sea shore, when I consider
things of tears like this. And by your reason,
my sneering critic, my words on the Word
are just the querulous whine of a Huck Finn
turned pedant. Probably wired-out thin on
beer-sodden french nihilism while dawn stars
dissolve in gray over Laguna or New Haven.
Toss them aside! Herewith, to wit, ends all your
professional obligation—go find your friends!

Last spring on a full-noted lenten eve,
azaleas abloom and somewhere I'm sure bucks
and bullocks starting and farting, I strolled
across Austin with three other Professor Poets
from, of all things, a creative writing teachers'
conference. (Though only true things like stones
in the midst of it all pulse with poetry,
we teach in school.) And at the statehouse
our bicker was too intent on academic sinecure
to pause before portraits of famous Texans
who'd chosen to pose for posterity
in both ruffian coonskin and the slicker's
stickpinned foulards. At the center
of that solemn pantheonic vastitude, we
enjambed our feet firm on a star to shout
up to a star in the dome. Our yells
shuddered down as ghost voices around
our heads. Surrounded by other stargazers,
whose soul-holes were also funneled toward
airy nothing, this scene resembled an ancient
beseechment, and also turkeys drowning in rain.

No matter what names, words, we cried up
to the star—animal/vegetable/mineral—all
fell back down as the same hollow groan:
WOE. And I recognized, of course, an occasion
for Modern longing. How Faust—white, middle-
aged and male as ourselves—felt the Word
run hot and cold in his striving. Or Forster's
cave-*boum*, or Chekov's orchard-twang, or
any other high-sign ambiguity we studied hard
in school so we could keep a sadness special
in secret codes, a loss more magical than dull
churls could know. *Boum*, spelt as Peter
Sellers as Inspector Clouseau says "bomb."

As a matter of fact, planted on that star,
I felt no longing—but because I'm not closed
in earnest grief don't assume I'm trapped
in the comic. Anyone would rather grope
after the numinous in a dark stone than stand
in the clanging glare of this store's
pinball aisles before the impossible fear
of the innocent. Blindly looking into the heart
of light. When I offer to hold her child
and calm its hullabaloo she says, "Mind your
own fucking business." And when I consider,
that's an honest reproof—Wisdom often runs
haggard in the streets. Yes, I see your know-
it-all leer, Mephistopheles! Some nut, huh?
Who just stands and waits there like Old Dan
Tucker, too late to get his supper . . . ?

That's my business. I'll keep making my offer,
but these tossed words—unseen, unheard
like famous trees or claws fallen to scuttle
floors of silent woods or seas—speak to no one.
I don't spend light on the lovers cocooned
in their mobilhomes, too wrapped in self-
absorbed coital anxiety to heed my vermiculate
syntax. For these, we pull and yank from between
the bony bars of our chests our own hearts
and right next to the Cheer and Shout boxes
offer them up, still warm and dripping. So
to speak. . . . But these words, dusty
from hopeless wrestling for the Word,
are given up to an even Higher Indifference.
Not the one some choose to name Art,
or Happiness, or Elvis but the one Milton
meant, who has no use for praise yet lets us
earn our healing in the labor of its singing.

Deer Season Again

—for Rob Patton

"Put your sweet lips just a little closer
to the phone ..." It was Old Jim Reeves
crooning low and slow again from down
in his dark throat where we suppose
the hurt is over all these years.
A blast from our hell-raising past
where we cannot dwell again and I
was humming and nodding and thumping
the wheel and even busting out in
snatches of it when a truck cut me off
and a doe gazed up through my windshield
with brown eyes immense with that famous
innocence and sweet trust we dreamed
on the faces of girls we secretly loved
when we groped through the dream mist
all hard and over-ready (oh boy
oh boy) for everyone's first time
in those dreams we had again and again.

But this tongue lolled out slimy
with blood. In fact, her whole head
nodded off the tailgate like the toy pup
with light-up eyes they put rearview
to match the bobbing of furry dice
from the mirrors. A gut-shot deer
in short and very shortly a pile
cruised past stacked head to asshole
and both holes muffed with dark crimson.
And then everywhere: draped over fenders

or curled like big cats on car-tops
and lashed to pick-ups' gunnels
with hooves poked stiff to the sky.
I sailed down the Oneonta road
a clear fourlane to Albany as Jim
growled that ending we always sang
along with long ago ... "and tell your
friend there with you he'll have to go."

I glimpsed a pair of hunters with their
shotguns jouncing like crazy as they hopped
the median ditch headed for greener woods.
"O *selva oscura*" I thought wincing at
at what an egghead wiseass I was but
still thinking. Their stupid Elmer Fudd
hats and vests were day-glo orange
instead of the fuzzy red checks they wore
twenty years ago that three a.m.
when they beat us up in Wes & Les's Diner
because you punched *My Boy Lollipop*
three times in a row on your quarter
or because we sassed back with fifty cent
words like Big Thinkers whatever in hell
those were but orange won't work better.

Some pimply kid will still get blown away
before his chance to get rubbed all over
with deer guts and goosed all around
for good luck. Your stupid song lisped
"He makes my heart go giddy-up"
while I mopped your nose gushing
like a virgin. "Are you happy now?"
I asked one-two-three times
until you said "Whatever this is
it is not happiness." I heard
your voice again clearer than

the radio: an interstate epiphany.
We weren't big brains. Who in hell
owned a sliderule? We thought we
were nothing. Weren't we crouched
to that same sticky counter as them
at the same nowhere hour hoisting
greaseburgers to our faces as the same
yellow cheese slithered from our squeeze?

Better to be nothing than them
we thought then but we'd been hunting
all night for that dripping meat
and I'll bet we've both leaned against
pick-ups since then with an evening beer
taking a moment from hacking up dust
to speak a few short words and poke
something dead in the truck bed.
Our hearts have always felt happier
in gory sunsets glowing us red
and orange than at cocktail parties
where a voice ceaselessly whines
that the mind under the mind
is the true mind and a shotgun
is therefore a penis. It is not.

We have but one mind and one heart
and the children of their anguish
are both cruel and tender. I saw
for the first and last time cruising
that highway flanked by cargoes
of death that we never could be happy
that all we have truly is a hot pursuit.

American Gogol

—*for Ronald Reagan*

Midsummer on the Midwest road: tidy hoboes
stand like sentries at every entrance ramp.
Only for a certain instant, a sudden space,
do their features focus; the rest is blur
as our Buick speeds abreast and by.

I hurtled forever forward
through the ragged, green flames of America,
chlorophyll flutterings in a vast, violet dusk.
My happy sigh wisped up with such a happy lip-
smack. "*O troika*, O *birdlike troika*,"
I whispered into Mozart's water music,
a feline purr of conditioned air. Our driver
steered with just one forefinger
on the quiet wheel, for some things
are miraculously easy here, so near to the end.

Yes, Gogol—Nikolai Gogol said it all
first. Our country bums travel fresh
as his simple serfs: khaki pants
and shortsleeves always starched and pressed
to knife-edge creases. Their withered skin,
red clay seams, hangs loose but thrifty
muscles bunch tight to the bones. One

I glimpsed had a piebald face and arms.
From some ancient scalding, I decided,
thinking as Gogol thought—puckish fancies.
An angry woman watched water and karo syrup

simmer for hours on the stove,
listening for his stumble on the stairs.
I saw patience, but no diffidence
in the thrust of his amber thumbnail.

Snoozing in crisp new-car redolence,
I wallowed in the wealth of my land,
lullabied by a pulse of tremulous jounces
and soft spurts of ecstatic momentum.
Hoboes flashed by, regular as phone poles,
darker in the bruised purple twilight.
It was cozy to imagine one extra of all
they wore in those brownpaper grocery bags
tucked in each armpit. Maybe sepia-tints
of their mothers—each in the same taffy-
brown dress, the same worried squint
into the same faded sun.

In delightful drowse, I was an embryo
cocooned at the core of a streaking star.
But in me another ember glowed. No,
my turn with love is over; no more
out in the weather, like the hoboes
with their slick hair raked back
in hopeful furrows. This dozing soul
could flare, be born again
at any moment to raze all dreams to ashes.

Wan Hope

—for Robert Pinsky

After we got suckered and lost the war
there weren't jobs or any place to roost,
so we just humped along close to the coast
scrabbling one day at a time. Now, on this
one evening, see? We've tied up the boat
and we're clanking down a vaulted hall
looking for dinner, a bath, maybe a girl
when Aeneas stops dead like he's been
coldcocked and starts juicing the inside
of his elbow with this noble flood of tears
and snot over nothing but pictures
on the wall. Then I see it too and I can't
believe my eyes! There's Anchises, Hector,
Priam—all of us, both living and dead
stiff as hell configured in the doing
of deeds. And the war just a few years old!
The rest of us just have to wait it out
while Aeneas blubbers over how beautiful
sadness is for about fifteen minutes,
dabbing at our eyes like a gnat's got in
there and all tensed up to an acute
knowledge that there's nowhere natural
to put your hands in this world. I'll tell
you the truth, doomed and gloomed as anyone
there, it was me who unfroze this poignant
tableau back on reel. Real casual I put
my arm on my pal, "How's that new helmet
liner, still chafing?" And in the echo
of our own hollow clanging, we walked on

15

then. "Tough-guy swagger," a critic might
say. "A wise-ass trivialization of human
grandeur and tenure revealing naught
but the poet's own spiritual paucity."
Whew! And wanly, my pale fish-hand in
a dazed drift up to the bait, I could
only say, "Well, at least I was there."

But that's crap; I wasn't there. This
part's been just a poem, a parable
meant so cold souls can't understand
and be forgiven. But now I'll tell
the story behind the story. A school pal
and I bartended fraternity parties
and at one in the pre-dawn wreckage
when only the team's star tackle
was left with his toxic fear and rage,
and his vicious sycophants, and two
highschool girls, deaddrunk, who
shouldn't have been there, those cruel
thugs told them to undress and beat
them when they wouldn't. My friend said,
"Hey, you bastards, leave them alone!"
and they beat us too. They cracked
his ribs and his jaw and made his gut
bleed. I fought hard until they re-broke
my nose and then—what the hell—
begged for mercy. They took the cutest girl
upstairs, clamped her neck in a windowsash
and ganged her from behind. We sat
out on the curb away from the light
under a sickle moon with the other girl
who just whimpered when we spoke
and wouldn't let us touch her. My pal
began to cry, a terrible weeping without
hope or dignity, and he beat his knuckles

on the asphalt. Then I said this, "Listen,
those girls should have known; we did
all we could." Which is crap, of course.

And I suppose on the blackboard of an ethics
course before a warm crescent of faces
some yellow chalk could screech this
so a rubber-tipped pointer could jab it:
accidie. Cowardice in greek, as doctors
always scribble names of sickness. The point,
again, is that I was there—again
and again and again in places so stupid
they're hidden not merely from cunning
but from wisdom itself. And I never saved
anyone for Love and Freedom and Art—
in fact, all those I drank and fought
with got turned to pigs and run off
cliffs. Even now, most of these I put
my arm around still smoke cigarettes
though every cough rumbles with warning
like a inscrutable parable, righteous
and merciless. My soul? It is like this:
a gray barmop, all sweetness soured
by shame, but no matter how sodden
with bitter spillage or the biles
that ferment with grief inside of men
you can wring this thing of tears again
and again. And whatever words I've said,
no matter how churlish and wrong, I meant
them for pity's sake and if I could I'd
soak all the world's anguish up inside
me and save the living and the dead.

Tremble

Not wind Poe-like tapping,
nor was I hunched hungover
in a black suit poised to versify
on the mildewed dead when a jet
too high for sight burst
through the skin of sound.
I knew that ka-boom
was just a flamboyant peel-out
for discreet dips and crests,
finally jostling through
my window pane so the clatter
sprung jazz in my glands
loose in my blood—
that and nothing more.

But I sat straight up too fast
from my noon snooze.
Fully clothed on a made bed,
I'd let silver amoebae squirming
in sun shafts mesmerize
my doze deeper than Whitman's
fecund loafing or even Poe's
clammy catatonia. Daystars
from my sudden sit-up faded
and I felt the pump chug—
that wet muscle slogging
circles in its slimy cage.
What old butterfly Beard,
or Edgar Poe without a wince
at literary distraction
would have called the heart.

18

Not valentines, pink buttocks
blossoming to delight Dr. Freud.

But when I heard the furnace
Click high in the housebeams
and the humid sigh hissing
from the vents ceased, it did
trigger a coincidental pause—
a metaphor and nothing more.
But that first tremor
surged closer with an inner
rumble that's so rarely felt
you can't forget, as near
as dead fingers that will tap
so suddenly a tremble elbows
through what I mean what I say
when I say the heart.

This Tree

said the little plaque in sober brass,
"replacing the beloved 'Stump'
is a gift from the Class
of 1977." Clearly a playful crowd,
and the tree is a ginkgo, coy fans
all aflutter, already heliotroping
hard to the east. Stump hell,
I remember that old elm,
stemming higher than slate roofs
to open wide to the sky full
of God. Before they all
got dutched. Well, to this tree
someone had tethered a half-grown
spaniel bitch with vinyl clothes-
line and gone off, to class
I guess. The black pool
on gray asphalt, thick drool
roping from her sweating tongue,
mirrored a ghostly flit
of shadows from those waving
leaves. Far away her steady bark,
like a handsaw's cry as it comes
and goes through cheap pine,
or that hammer we hear
wedging air with an anger
without heat, annoyed me.
For small dogs disgust me,
yet to let loose one so young
to lose herself would be
as cruel as to tie her in the sun.

I didn't think hard
for anyone before I retied
her in some scanty locust shade.
I was sweating and panting
and probably blushing all red
and stupid, holding the styrofoam
plate of water like a choirboy
and it still sloshed anyway
on the stairs and worn tiles
before the doors of a "Job Fair"
where the kids were all three-
pieced and talcumed, holding
big brown portfolios
and getting the hell away
from my spill and red face
and kneeworn corduroy smelling
of loss and sick dog.
But I thought two small thoughts
watching the puppy shlup-shlup
it up. My dad was born (1909)
the year the chestnuts died.
Cow that is, not horse. The ones
you can eat. Also how very much
I'd like to beat the shit
out of the smug prick or princess
who left this dog tied to that tree
in the full heat of this sun.
Because, I guess after all these
trees and stumps, which I never
thought to love, I'm still
not civil. In fact, probably
only lethargy and technical
boneheadedness keeps me
from mounting the famous clocktower's
winding stairs with a trombone

case full of grief. Ah hell,
I won't hurt anyone; it's just
a little hard here in this future
with its new trees and the sun
so bright my eyes water. I'll
tell you though: take all the trees,
I'll never love a god damn stump.

Cayuga Heights Crows

—for Archie

It's impossible not to hear
in the cackles of these crows
a human jeer. Not like kids
circling some runt at recess,
taunting out his tears—
those cries are high and clear
as horns. The calls of these
enormous crows sound phlegm-
sodden, like old boys on a store
porch laughing at the tears
of a kid whose dog they've kicked.
Big as buzzards, they blackened
the top of a blood-red maple
and their yells reminded me
of a bad smell. Down home boys
shoot them to save the beans
and corn and for fun. And I was
shocked to think I thought that:
"down home," I mean. I thought
about your words on crows. How
this village isn't zoned for crow-
shoots, but for stationwagons
squashing half-tame squirrels
on these almost country roads,
so they grow huge and brassy
on the mapled lawns. I mean
the crows. No stores here either
with stoves or barrels or fly-
blown screens but we know where.

Black or white those old boys
are always passing for a hit
the smallest bottle sold
and feeling kind of mean.
But I'm going to quit
seeing what I know in crows
to look hard at what is true.
In crows, I mean. That shotgun
sure made the air jump though.
Like a sudden haze of flies
glistening up far off yonder
off something really ripe
below the johnson grass.

East Polk Street Park

—for Pat Screen

To wrestle the padlock around for the key,
I must hunch stiff and low,
elbows tight to my sides, for poison sumac
nods turgid and trembling with venom
over me and its fingers, evil *fleurs de lis*,
with a most casual caress can raise
weltering blisters, hot tears turned acid.
A child might love that cozy cave,
with its dank stink of fat worms and chlorophyll
and you might sigh for the freedom, stepping
through chainlink out into the park's mowed grass,
rich sun buttering a civilized geometry
of softball diamond and jungle gym.
But I peeked through the links before I
stepped from my backyard to another country
to be sure the junkies weren't slouched like buzzards
on the little bleachers under the sweetgum tree,
for even their eyes say murder. One has hair
tied in brutal little knots, like tufts of spikes
bristling on the stinging buckmoth caterpillar.
He is goat-eyed—his pupils are black
slashes, rectangles centered in blank gray.
One time another be-bopped on the balls
of his feet, low hands flailing imaginary
snares and cymbals, to where I was
raking leaves and there unzipped and pissed
not four feet from where I stood so I could
smell his bitter urine glittering and drip-
ping off diamond fence rungs and broad

green viburnum leaves. His eyes, full on
me, were sleepy-lidded like a male lion's
as he shook the last drops from his cock.

So, I turn quickly to my tour, prying back
fence scrub with a long stick,
for stiff-coiled snakes may blend in weedhusks.
I peer, all the way to the interstate's corner,
for escape holes they snip with big clippers
made just for bike chains. Then I hurry
to slash and tear at wisteria vines
and tree limbs that might give a hand-
hold over barbed wire to *my* land.
Embarrassed by cowardice, my work is too
hasty: the sawblade snatches in the groove
with each yank; I twist and wrench branches
before the cuts are through. My spine
tightens at the fourlane's constant moan,
like lost souls' shredded cries plunging,
or hurtling by in eternal firewind.
Even a truck's downshift booms and groans
like a huge iron door slamming
on a far-off voice, in hopeless gloom.
No goon would snip passage into *that* wilderness,
but from my backyard's farthest corner
such a crazed barrage of sudden thwacks explode,
adrenalin fires in my veins like the hoodlums'
junk must hum in their first rush. It is my old
black neighbor, come out to help me chop, though
these last three years we've only known each other
as shapes and colors through his honeysuckle screen.
My startled scream provokes his foghorn bellow
and after one mute gaping moment of deaf gaze,
we both laugh the same stale wind of reprieve.

Not brotherhood; at bottom fear
is all we hold in common and we never
name that word. We're both scared by beasts
who spray their scents about the boundaries
of this park and then lounge back to watch us
slink and cringe in the corners of our vast
caged world—this world where fear
makes us each others' keepers, or witnesses
shivering in strewn glass and rain,
submitting like befuddled King Lears
to a halloween third degree of light and siren.
King Lear? This dignified old man, iron
moustache and sedate gardening trousers
he once wore to church, would be bewildered
by an allusive joke on "Mending Wall." And you?
Do you know that Frost was named for General Lee
and James Knox Polk was just Jackson's puppet
for a term? My own thoughts encircle me
like a wearisome fence I peer along and along
and as in nightmare, I seem to speak to ones
who hear or see right through me. I know
Polk died the same year as Edgar Poe,
Wordsworth one year later, and it makes no
sense the way we name our streets and parks.
The sky seems the same deep blue, bringing
always to mind the sea, and our grass
is the same pleasant carpet it always was
but at this moment which has been the same
and only moment, there is now nothing
but savage sun, the echoing whine of speed
itself and every gaze is as dead as a daytime
moon.

Spit

At the southwest corner of our town's white
marble bank where the old men sharpened
their knives grinding its edge down so it
looked like sucked sugar a red-nosed ex-
cop with milky eyes guarded every door
because "the vaults were stuffed with silver
the miners sweated for" or so our beatnik's
song said and at that spot we liked to arc
like shooting stars silver bullets
of sullen spittle well over the sidewalk
into our town's gutter because the corner
cop kept his eye yellow as the august
moon sharp on us to see that not one
slimy wad hit where some decent citizen
in a suit and shiny shoes might step or even
slip on those truculent gobs of wrath—lead-
gray like rich whalepuke nasty as spent semen
summoned with the same scrape of phlegm
that introduces some exact word in german
for how we felt slouching there if we'd
read books about it instead
of just spitting but not snapping—let
me make most definite—fingers
or shuffling our feet singing shoobie-
doobie or any cute shit like that
but just waiting one long rasp of steel
across stone per second to go in the navy
and listening between our ears to a suck
of smoke streaming through dead leaves
already knowing the tones of one hundred
and eight different carhorns and yes

that faintest pop—most fleeting fragrance
of a tiny bubble mashed deep in a wad
of gum—air burst back to air like
maybe the sound of a soul going home ...
No, that's too high-flown. It's like when
you step off the bus and look right at
the spot on the platform where your girl
stood on tiptoe tasting like juicyfruit
with her hand thrilling the sharp stubble
on the back of your neck so a small tic
shoots in your eye and you swallow hard
and heft your duffle into the new day
rising fresh in two hundred and seven
windows and stride off in the direction
of silver you already see flashing on
the cop's chest eleven blocks away.

Greyhound/Science Fiction

A fresh bus in Syracuse filled fast
with squeaky-clean Kyotan Bourgeoisie.
Each mama and papa-san wore a bright
orange blazer, a turquoise company
badge on each hankie pocket. Ecstatic
squeals, gutterals, with snaps from
many cameras drowned the air conditioner's
endless, listless exhale. The tinted
windows, already trembling from the motor's
idle, were shocked by alien presence,
fauve reflections writhing round our heads.
So, he sat by me, the only other white
American aboard who talked his lingo.
And he would know right off the bat
if I knew we're visited by superior beings
from distant galaxies? Of course I did,

I said, for all the supperless hours,
the careening miles, loneliness of torn
vinyl and crackling intercom had addled
loose my one lick of sense. He told
a secret he'd told so many times,
his voice held an uncomprehending reader's
steady, flat despair. How the car froze
shut on a pitchblack, empty road.
How he and a wife now gone were beamed
up into the silver humming glow,
stripped and painfully probed by some
big-headed ones—all yellow and hairless.
How a disemboweled dog, its pitiful
human collar still dangling tags,

was spread in mute gore on a winking
table. How they awoke nude and broken
in the cowflop of some farmer's field.

No matter how insistently I offered up
my faith, the hopeless eye he fixed on me
would not glitter. He was cursed to tell,
not listen, and the windy echoes whistling
through his starved heart would have drowned
out all answering cries across the bleak strand.
And what was I? A vain little peacock who
oh so casually dropped the titles
of my skinny volumes. And that raised him
to say he lacked the "way with words"
to warn our world and I'd get ten percent.
This commercial vision enthralled him so,
he barely noted the busdriver's braying
hullabaloo when an oriental elder
stripped for pajamas in full aisle-view
thirteen miles from Binghamton.

But I told my new friend no: another earthly
story kept grinding in my brain. It seemed
too sadly predictable that golden strangers
throbbing with soft light would not come
to save us from ourselves, but to behave
just like our own geewhiz-flyboy scientists.
The true knowledge I hungered to discern
and tell is why when I "rode the hound"
from coast to coast I saw a fat woman
slap a weeping child in every midnight
station. And why can bookstores no longer
sell Conrad's journeys into the secret heart?

Why, I asked this man, does only "how to jog,"
or, "how to be rude with equanimity to sad

little men on buses" turn the cost-efficient
buck? And please tell me why worlds so far
away, only the beams of their extinct suns
persist, seem closer than Benares where
mothers maim their own wee babes
like bonsai trees to improve success
in beggary? I told this witness how
I longed with all my heart and soul to believe
in voices from blazing shrubs, in angels
and demons who swoop good simpletons
up aloft so their frantic feet would kick
helplessly for the fields they had just
cursed through a veil of sweat.

What was his reply to this unbaring
of my secret self? He turned his face
to its frozen double in the window glass.
He had more sense than to talk to creeps
on the public buses.

December 18th, 1944

On the day of my birth General McAuliffe said "Nuts."
Without doubt he meant my sexual prowess
would be prodigious. It is certain the German
    Command,
both high and low, did not understand.
Those girls and wives of my past and those yet to be,
yet to meet, were embryonic—ignorant of destiny.
Those lucky ladies! They have often thought I was
"the nuts" and told me so always
to my face. Yes, NUTS—a meaty, versatile, after-
    dinner
expletive. No other could be plainer
and still say less in modest prophecy of a mind's
    nobility,
like the infant's first defiant squall.
To every earthly duty I grow with this dictum in
    humility,
from little acorn to the knottiest oak of all.

Negative Incapability

When dreams turn mean
or unbearably beautiful
custom counsels a pinch
and I snatched at my pink self
like a monkey in an anthill.
But what could go wrong in Eden
where just us two mooned buck-
naked, yet oddly unshy, in clover
swaying in a buzz like drunk snakes?
Dreams never say "ought" or "This
is truth." Action starts in mid-
scene and you know, somehow,
what you know so I knew it was you,
really you, inside your best
friend's skin. Whoever ... Who
cares? In the desolate slosh
of a vast ocean in the endless black
of the universe a smallest thing
glows and is gone—that's a dream!
Lookit—one flick of my michelangelo
finger and you surfed full-blown
from my rib on a clam shell.
God rarely showed, and then
costumed as a bonfire or small wind—
no real substance. It was understood
that I was pretty much in charge,
that my job came first. Namely:
to name each sticky spasm
into meaning. It all felt so right—
daisies, cornflowers, tiny aster
twinkles blooming at my blessing

with small grunts and sighs. I could
do no wrong and got too good,
I guess. My right hand
would command four hectares
of blood-red poppies to blush
open in symphonic hemorrhage
while my left paired lambs
with lions. But even right there
in the best it ever got
I felt this lonesome heartburn.
Some gloomy german would name it
just right but it's more down
to earth to just shrug and grin—
awshucks—and call it horny.
God had just drifted by the garden
dressed out as the aurora
borealis when two plump snails
in blissful piggyback scooted
a froth of iridescent bubbles
right over our bare feet. In dreams
and on camping trips placental mucus
isn't so disgusting and before
real estate and shame it never
seemed stupid to say something
like "behold." "Behold," I said,
"Your least creeping slime
are given to be fruitful."
I knew God pretty well by then.
A man of few words—taciturn,
grouchy and prone to imperatives:
"Good!" "Bad!" No direct input,
but you could buzz his bonnet.
And, boy!—you were some doll
to behold! Never will I forget
the rose filigree vein-work
lacing your shyer nipple, or

the demure riffle of venus
hair bending to the moist pants
of that sirocco breeze. Ah,
there was time for detail
in that smaller universe.
Wedged in all four corners of it,
pouchy zephyrs puffed perfumed
melodies all night long.
Knowing nothing right or wrong,
we fondled the whole world—
pasta-poor in cramped quarters,
our eyes sappy with happiness
locked over a candle flame.
I got you a shepherdess crook,
a pink-bowed prop, and put you
(oh so petite and goosebumpy)
on a knoll so you could better
watch me strut my stuff.
But you loved you the best.
I just knew. No need to dream
up the snake, the fruit,
the nude crouch in the thicket
while our father boomed down
the path. . . . No need for blame,
doom programmed from the git-
go in the primal chromosome.
Skin for skin, let it suffice
to say we can pluck ourselves
from dream to dream but paradise
where we're stuck is wilderness.
Enow?

Idle Tears

"Deep as first love, and wild with all regret;
O Death in Life, the days that are no more!"

On the seashore, waves' moist crashes
harmonized the flow. Gulls' crazy little
shrieks, so peculiarly fierce with lament
and shrewish nagging, seemed response
enough. It was all so big there: clouds,
water, even invisible wind heaved around
the way huge things will; corresponding
so well with sourceless rumbles and surges
within us. It was so easy to just throw
something on then without clashing.

As easy as it's now hard. For idle grief,
that whimsical splurt of hot saline
from *je ne sais* where, has drifted out
of rage again. O a good-cry is still
hygienically purgative, in fact
more than ever in groups. But obsessive
blubbery can betray an excess of moral
seasoning, so quizzical furrows
crinkle the brows of potential lovers
and/or employers. "Really?" they ask,
and "Interesting" they interject
in that way that says they're thinking
"Too intense!" Which is worse than dandruff.

For what should Divine Despair be,
except the name of an ice-cream flavor
in Woodstock, Vermont? In fact,

even the pharisees who insist that our
best-gasped words bubble from no source,
that our smeary pages hold only sign-
scribbles for their alchemic mysteries—
even they insist that every sob
must serve as system within systems.
Not much anymore do we saunter hand
in hand under the droning elms
on a summer's eve over to the college
to moon away a lecture. In fact,

my particular crowd feels more comfortable
these days at the less-nice beaches
where radios blare always loud and not
quite tuned. Fat, balding men in street
clothes drink beer from cans, stare at girls
and spit on the sand there. Or they fold
their tattooed arms and glare at the sea.
You can stand there too to daub your eyes.
In these places they still don't care why
you feel bad. No one bothers you if you act
like you're mopping sweat and don't get snooty.

Impatience

"Curse God and die," she said
and slammed the door so hard
the whole damned trailer shook.
What was I supposed to do?
Squat in busted dishes
scraping my sores? Roll in ashes
licking like a sick pup and rip
my clothes to shreds like I once
popped buttons off my shirts
in drunken tantrums? Oh yeah,
I floated loose in some fine
raiments once, slapping green
grease on palm after palm.
Walk up and down on that earth
awhile—you'll see it's skin
for skin, man, pain for gain.
All lunches paid in full. And so
she's gone, the woman who urged
me on to greater sin. Gone
with car, cash and plastic magic.
Hunching to morning juice and joint
I circle job ads. But it's no use.
Ten's almost noon—too late
to scrape up a happy face, press on
a monkeysuit to peddle my paper.
Friends drop in to peer
for loose beers in a yellow shaft
of curling fog. They jab stained
fingers at my vainest crimes hovering
in the blue haze of their Luckies.
Why listen? What's right but failure

to do wrong? Mother never hid
that my conception was accident.
I watch my watch until they go.
At one hour in each day
in this eastern standard place
a man and woman, young and restless,
lie in a bed they've made. Too
sick with sin to love, they say
the word often. My eyes alone
see them writhe one on one,
knead each other's skin like bread.
My ears ring with their cries;
my eyes burn with their tears
and a whirlwind churns in my mind.
I curse that first squall of light
that fell on the glistening slime
of my birth. I keep a face calm
and hard as a potato but my heart
rejoices for the fact of death.

The Giants' Game

"Never overkick your coverage."
This voice drawls out of a snazzy blazer,
but it never went to our school. No,
that accent growls from "Hardknocks You,"
as our old drill sergeant called the fear
that taught him to be cruel. And this voice
also mushes marble-mouthed on the vowels,
is fond of simple wisdom in well-placed
consonantals, cracking off like carbine
rounds. Our Sarge was hardscrabble
mean, not kindly under his crust. Salt
that blights the earth, in fact.
Our voices changed. We learned to bark
and snarl in our sleep and fresh
from Officer's School we ordered the five
hundred into some steamy valley, confident
the pep of games mattered more than lives
so safe they'd only get real after school.

So, as the game keeps exploding to squirm
in two colors on the screen, why do us
couch potatoes give the voice and its snappy
adage the cynic's snort? It's an easy
snicker if you've made no kicks to cover.
After twenty years, we should surely
"recontext intrahistorically" our text-
book war. That fall push for Petersburg,
so eager for the winning kill ratio
new ghosts lacing our morning breaths
went unnoticed. Horse shadows stretched
back west a little thinner at each

twilight and fewer dogs tailed our train
each dawn. Nor did it seem strange
we only loved each other, living and dead
the same, as if we'd never thrown out
the pictures we found in our wallets
when we bought them. O, many a storm-
tossed year passed before we groped
the cold stones of our home shores,
just in time for our boyhood dogs
to die of joy in our arms.

We sneer at all voices paid to proclaim
the play by play of games in odic
baritones. The ecstasy of feats done
for *aes alienum:* brassy praise
for another man's coin. Since Sportsfan
Pindar, they've sung on the heaves
and grunts of boygods and giants,
where only a win makes it real. Our own
words are snug as satin rosepetals—
roses to deaden the clods as they fall.
For this sneer sits like a canker,
an ulcer festering at the core. Whenever
a kicked ball soars to wobble
in the aching silence of its sublime
peak, we taste a regret cold and bitter
as coins they put on the tongues
of the dead to buy them into heaven.

Beholding Nothing

You've got to have a mind like nuclear winter
to watch slush slide to thud off a pinebough
assuming its acid and ready to slither
with salt down gutters and gurgle through
sour pipes busted deep in blackest places
by the earth's small shrugging often reminding us
of restless anguish; it's just water seep though

and you have to have been melting a long time
a lot faster than a frozen heart could fathom
to not panic sipping the last ellipse of wine
as cognac uncorks clearing your throat to whine
how the land and the wind and the winter sun
whisper grim secrets to you the only listener
unlistened to in the candles' sooty glitter

so you murmur doom and love to the babysitter
about that bomb while she just snaps her gum
like a few leaves crackling in latest autumn
while streetlight licks her hair in cold flares
as she regards in black glass a pure reflection
of everything that's there or ever need be there.

Inflation

Since wages must be earned
sin pays no wages. Yet we know
what the grim slogan means
we once saw on barns
and billboards driving everywhere.
But no more. Why?
Because now we know it all?
Of course not. We jog daily
against death and we still
confess even to strangers
all our sins to relieve
stress in those chambers
of our hearts. Yes, secrets
hiss from us as so much
harmless steam. But it's no
good. A sour gas stays
and squeezes in our chests.
So we've lifted the message
from the pastures
where it was fading in the sun
and pasted it on the very cars
themselves. In fact never
has it meant more—
This senseless death
we're supposed to pretend
to love this hideous God for.
As if our secret sins
were just some stolen items
we could hide in our clothes
like the genitals that shame
us so. But to keep those
we'd curse God and die without
a thought.

Oh, Oh

My girl and I amble a country lane,
moo cows chomping daisies, our own
sweet saliva green with grass stems.
"Look, look," she says at the crossing,
"the choo-choo's light is on." And sure
enough, right smack dab in the middle
of maple dappled summer sunlight
is the lit headlight—so funny.
An arm waves to us from the black window.
We wave gaily to the arm. "When I hear
trains at night I dream of being president,"
I say dreamily. "And me first lady," she
says loyally. So when the last boxcars,
named after wonderful, faraway places,
and the caboose chuckle by we look
eagerly to the road ahead. And there
poised and growling are fifty Hell's Angels.

Peach Pit

The dried seed sucked clean
long ago clattering in the close
corners of my car ashtray looks
like an elfin brain even
shaped for a pointed cranium
and calcified in pyre ashes
and unseen for a million
years until these sudden sunrays
beaming through the splash
of autumn maples flicker
shadows across its stolid ripples.

Its fleshy convolutions
will darken like October
leaves above darkened unseen
which is how a blood pool thickens
mounded in its black skin
or the way a stain seeps its way
over and then into a wall pattern.

There are many ways to say it
and words twist hopeless
to persuade yet mean no surcease
of mind or heart when I say it
is no brain but a seed

its shell coiled in whorled rings
to grip flesh that has now gone
back to dust or ashes but
I think wet meat still sings
unseen inside like they said the moon

and stars once did for elfin ears
and if I flung it to clatter
across roadside pebbles it could
scuttle for darkness and unseen
split like a brain or broken
heart to unfurl a turgid stem
into June sun always new again.

In Each Day

—for Lisa Ress

Orders came, precise, he said,
not to stack them, but you know
how it is. On the planes sometimes
they came piled, but he always laid
them end to end on the carts.
Canvas mummies, always stiff and quite
easy to swing out and down. Planes
often came at dawn when a thin
silver streak seeped up from
where the sea was. When they cut
the engines he sometimes smelled
salt and kelp in the new quiet.
But most often the motors idled
as they checked tags and hauled
bodies out into that sucking howl.
At the center of the roar a constant
whistle rose and fell
like a shriek. And he could not
hear that scream for long, he said,
and not go mad. And he did not.
Sometimes you must handle the dead
like baggage and at another time
cradle one in your arms. Neither time
is as good or bad as you think.
Like looking on the lost children
on this morning's milk carton—
gone so long they would be grown
except you know in someone
somewhere, all the time

drones a sound that cannot end.
As the first coffee wound
your stomach tight you did not hear
the birds in the quiet of your thought.
Their steady warble that shakes
each single new day loose
as we ready for our grim business.

At Susanne's School

High on its knoll
the flag rolls up to a snap
over and over, a growl
and pop in ceaseless wind
like one burp after another.
The wind's gnawed its edges
soft, whipped lint
aloft in breeze and it tears
along the bars, almost up
to the box of stars.
So they observe a rite
at Susanne's school:

Her grade lines up by height
before the pole; her yellow hair
streams up into silken knots.
They sing the song and say
the pledge and think the silent
thought. And down she comes,
an old dust-rag's flounce
with every yank and clank.
Fifty-four wide eyes, I think,
reflect its burn and they bury
it, a painted coffee can for urn,
like a pet or some poor dead bird.
The new flag's quiet;
its sober ripple is sedate
and its fresh swash of red
doesn't seem to mind
the wind. One can almost
hear the grainy pencil scrawl
behind black panes that mirror
an eternal shifting glare.

At the Jet Show

These look like manta rays.
Like they'd cruise the green curve
of a stratospheric coral reef; for
after they've banged past their own boom,
they cut so fast through nothing they seem
to float in fish silence. They're nothing
like the balloon-winged planes
I drew in school. I lined arrowheads
across triangles, pinning the yellow
paper with an elbow and clamping
my tongue in my teeth to steady
a shaking in my blood. Stars took shape
while the teacher's talcum croon
lulled us to torpid cloudland. In that hum
my chest fattened with Honor & Duty.

In the grey old movies where music
yelped or groaned as it started, the grins
on those fighter pilots were wild curves
as they slid from cockpits, tossing back
long scarves and cowlicks. How beautifully
they loved life, patting Betty Grable's
fanny and roaring off to death.
Always they had a chocolate bar to toss
to little sloe-eyed Dondi as they strode
across the tarmac into oblivion.
Grown now so I seem to float
almost silent in the midst of my life
hurtling past me, there seems no lovely
way to die. These almost wingless planes
are beautiful like sleek and terrible fish,
but I could never love them, or these new

pros swaddled like mummies in their space
cocoons. No, not with the fat heart
I had high on the baler seat in my uncle's
lucky leather jacket with the dragon
on the back, making the engines groan
and scream in my throat, in oblivion ...

These were made for the perfect silence,
an eternal glide above the fallout.
They'll flank some moviestar president's
capsule, peacefully spinning tomb,
far above a winter light where scarabs
will be unfolding their new wings,
probing from crevices the new humming
in the air.

Catfish Grumble

—for J. S. Borck

A sudden strain, like a blow.
I hauled my cane-pole high
and a catfish ripped out through
the bayou's placid murk.
He flexed on invisible line,
whiskers goring air like
a midget bull. They can live
in our air forever
and a blurb I'd read rose
out of my mind's empty hum:
"His losses never lose heart."
It snagged in there like a snatch
of song you can't shake loose.

I admit to a slight lessening
of heart when his cotton white
belly spun to confederate
gray. Channel cats are so mean
to skin and all catches must
be kept and eaten. Only
if I keep that moral law
will polefishing keep its meaning.
Catfish will talk to men,
complaining with low grrs
and grumbles and this one's
gritty murmur went "wedge-
wedge-wedge" so plaintively
it ached my heart. But even
alone there I wouldn't show it.

He thumped about the boat's tin
bottom as my hand slunk round
him like a jackal flanking
a pawing buck. At each half-
hearted foray, he cocked
a wicked backspine loaded
with wake-up juice. Grappling
that slime was like a sex dream
with a succubus and when
I pinned his satin squirm
between my boot and leather
workglove, I lost even more
heart. While my pliers probed
for the hook, the word "shit"
hissed out at every breath—
toneless litany of any dullwit,
luckless and weak of heart.

I guess I wasn't a real Southern
poet. Those rough sports are soul-
brothers to the critters they kill.
Their huge hearts surge as warm
and golden as bourbon lighting
the bar where they rest damp heads
in brawny arms to weep
their warrior tears. If loss
trenches in the heart, how can
the mind forget? Sobs still sway
the fringes on their coats
to the exact tempo of the video-
game's brazen honks and bleats.

Fitful thrashing from the ice-chest
startled me. Though a high noon
sun bent my head into heat
billowing back out of the metal

54

boat and the brown path it had
meandered through duckweed sparkled
a silver too bright to look at,
I shivered. My mind saw the sad
slither of his milky belly
over sunfish stiff as wedges
from store ice. As if an orange
glow from their smothered throats
could light his passage. I read
about a Northern catfish
unthawed from a block of lake
ice that bumped its head against
the sides of the galvanized tub,
ready for another life. Their numb
hearts just cannot quit. Because

I was sober and sun-sick and alone
with only this fish and because
in the midst of man's life
there is a bomb in his chest,
I paddled for the buttonwood
shade where the water was smoothed
as black and quiet as bottom mud
and cottonmouths looped in cypress
roots with such heavy-fleshed
inertia it seemed impossible
that a bobber's sudden plunge
could uncoil them like whips,
or like a hand's fast fumble
for a bursting heart. And despite
the wedge in my heart, I nailed
his head to a tree and skinned him.

The Jungle Gym

The game was to catch the girls
and cage them in the jungle gym.
They fanned out like geese,
running with those funny flounces
and squawking in happy consternation.
Thrilled on by their Sabine squeals,
our hunting yelps went guttural
and by the time we'd caught them,
one at a time, we'd become too mean
to grin back at their banter.
Bigger than us then, they feigned
a haughty docility as we strutted them
to their pen. We got just a mite
too proud, perhaps. A boy always got
too rough and a girl always cried.
It was a game with girls, like the radio
said love would be and the thing to do
with games was always win.
The teacher in her no-nonsense voice
told the glitter of fierce eyes
clustered tight to a hurt sniffle,
"No one made you play that game."
That is one reason we rarely heed
the voice of reason. What should
she do? Sit alone with a few pale
others where crackled leaves pile
in the sandbox corner? The small

boy guarding girls, caged by open poles
and bars, steamed in perpetual blush,
he felt so honored by their taunts.

He felt a reason he couldn't say yet
when one shrieked and, gawky, winced
away from her own noise.
He felt an itch inside his chest
like he'd felt under the cast
on his broken arm. It was the game
that made them honorbound to stay
inside the jungle gym with him
he knew, but he was honored anyway.
Honored they flashed their eyes
at him, the smallest, from that place
where he went all alone in the druid
quiet to lie on packed dirt and gaze
through bars and poles where clouds
roared by in silence. A square of sky
where if he could just lie
through all the scudding seasons,
all the right stars, bye and bye,
would glitter on him, one by one,
as if by reason.

The Tongue

This pink tongue flops
across the park green
panting like a hot engine
ardent with dumb joy.
With each jolting wag, white
slather flies in the sun.
Through pruned hemlocks
the tongue weaves. It
jounces a raw pink peekaboo
in and out white phlox clusters,
skids down the dirt path
and plunges in the spring pool
to slosh up scoop after
cold scoop of black
water. A naked muscle
thrusting from its bundle
to flex and twist in steady,
strong strokes. Remembering
how raspy tongue buds
aroused your leg's fine down
in a lingering, exquisite
swipe, a snail's silver
passage, you might name it
Joy. Yes, it lolls
its drooling love upon
your lap so you coo to it,
prickled pink by wet obeisance
in its eyes: O wuff, O cruel
wuff! For you could also call
it Sorrow. Dripping here
eagerly proffered is all

you asked for and something's
still missing. Shadowed
in such ingratitude, how can
even the sun warm your bones?
In wrong, even this tongue
slinks in naked shame. Like us
once, dripping pink in wilderness.
Is that why cynic means dog-like?

Kipling at Southsea

Grown up you brandished courage words
for the crown and lion on the coin
and swaggered under a white man's burden.
But often in a dream you woke small
again in your boyhood bed at Southsea.
From a gentle bob in deep blue sleep
loomed the sour widow your mother
left you with. Black as a thunderhead,
come to beat you for your daily sin.
Her moon-wet eyes glinted white against
the night's blue murmur like the frog's
stomach, splayed and bulging, you poked
in the pond scum. "For Jesus's pain,"
she said and struck you. Hard.
Because you strutted about her baptist
house with your boasts and curses
like a languid rajah boy, despite
the placard that said LIAR on your chest.
By the dream's end you'd always grown
hard as a man again.

With her stiff palms flat above her
head and her bosoms big as melons
jouncing with every blow, she looked
like goddess Devi when she danced for Siva
on the temple frieze your dusky servant
sneaked you off to see. He'd wagged
a stiff brown finger up to the Divine
Ones twining in serpentine ecstasy
and winked one wet eye, half-lidded
with sleepy pleasure. "No tell Memsahib,"

he'd said. But Mummy must have known
your lie. For on that Southsea shore
she knelt and pressed you deep and hard
into her furs' tea and curry smells,
and walked away. Forever. Over grey sand,
beyond the grey sea always rolling in
from the sky's grey end.

Because the black widow's musky rage
smelled sweet as milk creaming in the sun
and wild as frog slime you sniffed
furtively on sticky fingers,
you got stiff in that dream every time.
You ached to rub the itch of tears
on your red, wet face across nipples,
you knew budded pink and firm
beneath her sour wool. No, not there
but in your black mind the evil
swarmed out like night vermin sniffing
the patchouli stench of her boy's
pomade. In or out, a black air swirled
as viscous and oily as hell's own soot.
The sting from her sharp slaps would soften
to a glow of hot caresses. In rigid shame
you heard your sister sobbing for your pain.

And then the worst. Hopeless straining
with all your mustered Will, fierce
little Englishman, against traitor flesh.
But it pushed itself deep, panting hard
into the soft bed until you burst with sin
murmuring "Mummy, Oh Mummy" again and again
in such hard despair and loathsome pride.
She would never come back to you.
"Be strong, my little rajah Ruddy,"
was her last warm breath in your ear.

But a perfume swirling in your mind
made you weaker, and so more vile
than the least slimed creature born
to die for nothing in the muck. So
forever you curled into your core,
warm and unchanging as the panther's
blue fur under her eyes' sleepy, yellow
glitter. The brave orphan forever,
harder than any man. Savage and pure,
swinging your brown legs from the cannon
Zam-Zammah, you could never betray her
again. No, never.

The Popsicle Scepter

On a perforated plastic stick
he raised aloft a frozen confection
the royal purple of grape
commercial confiture
lightly frosting on the summer
air like a cattail whitens
to fluff in sun and wind
while he intoned *a basso*
on the heads of kids
in that curse/bless-me voice
of throne and pulpit
stage and screen the emperor
poem lingering on the word
"concupiscent" and went on
to recite the conjugation
of ice cream winking narrowly
at the irony of imaginary
signs alone differing inert
from active verb and noun
or glee from anguish
but they were of the age
(ah you know this age)
when all is shame and wished
he wouldn't mug and strut
around a public place
confabulating with the air
and told him so right then
and there like old conjugal
rights or wrongs sprung up
(O bitter Confiteor)
like dragonfangs to rebuke him

into silence where he lapsed
like a philosophic clown
mopping up a last stain
of light in a murmur of ghosts
but he did scream in there
alright like you and we all
once screamed for ice cream
which is yes sweet innocence
that was or seemed and is
more therefore—no much more—
than colored water's cold drip
for why else would he or you
or all of us in private places
rage and weep like the royal fool
who froze all he loved
with one stupid single touch?

Scallops in Garlic Sauce

Even roasts and chops come
roughly in the shape of the beast
but this bleach-white lozenge
poised to plop in my mouth
which is shaped to yawn
or cry out as well as eat
is too perfectly round to have come
from a loving God and because

I can't stop loving you

which I would play on the jukebox
if there was one—like there was
in the restaurant after our wedding
that the bar drunks punched
the Green Beret Song on all night
and glared at us though you were so
beautiful in your snowwhite suit
and your blonde hair shaped
like Jackie did hers—and because

my mind's made up to live in memory

this scallop dripping sexy sweet
sea-spice and wisping a tiny ribbon
of steam which might be some sort
of soul floating to some heaven
for all I know will most surely
just be ashes on my tongue—
unswallowable—

O be still my heart

I whisper into white meat
and God's all too human stink
all alone with me now
in all this sound and light where
each blow thuds louder
in my dry mouth so I fear
the gore-gnawing dogs stirring
from long slumber at my mind's far
corner and I tell you once
roused one can only yearn for
the quiet of enormous darkness.

A New Laugh

I would learn a new laugh
for your leaving. Walk far
away from this "Hunh-hunh-
hunh"—each snort nestling
a gob of sweet and trusting
phlegm. Adenoidal fawn bleats,
ingenuous puerile glucosity:
a laugh gaping a moist shelf
of pink and purple underlip
on life's heaves and buckles
to say "Jeepers!" in a shot-
gun plosion of double-bubble
spittle on the consonantal.

No more Mr. Nice Boy!
Compliant cuckold! I will
craft a chuckle wry and dry.
A cackle to clatter off
empty walls bitter as a chic
aperitif wrung from radioactive
cranberries with a pinched
to death lime-twist bloating
in its sediments. A laugh
to slice through all laughter
as a thin blade pares
the sides off a gaping fish
in quick, glinting strokes.

Wedged in the briefest silence
between a final cough in a dark
hall and the baton's fall

in a flood of light, or over
water dancing and the squeals
and gabble at the duckpond,
or even in your dreams'
fuzzy chromotints as you sigh
and smack your lips and burrow
deeper into some armpit's
synthetic musk, you will hear
my new laugh and think, "Never
did he laugh like that with me!"

Salt Treatment

As brine rinsed white over my mushy gums
stinging loose black blood-rot creviced
in my teeth, I thought of those Greek rocks
washed by a ceaseless ebb and seeth—
a wanderer's hand trembling from the surf. . . .
And I thought no act, however mean,
lacks paradigm. The thought made me wince,
as in shame for the nasty kiss or pasty meals
that fouled my mouth. I woke on another
morning with the boozy squeeze of sorrow
in my gut. Squinting up into the far blue
away from the buzzing glare *sur plage*,
I poked a stubble spike clean through
my foot. Oh my yes, my great scream
froze still the heat shimmers. They gathered,
moaning and clucking their bad news as they
always float in when someone's in hospital
or staked onto a rock. And as I lay
cursing God for the grit already rimming
the gore's ragged edge, the stern woman
with hair stiff as snakes and sparkling
with salt stepped from their murmur to say
with her arms black against the heavens,
"Bathe your wound in the sea." Oh yes,
they chanted, in the sea, the salt sea.
As I sank into the spume, pain sucking
all lights and colors within my airy skull,
the happy shrieks of children dashing from
a pounce of gentled waves, and the seagull's
tough jeer over clumps of distant kelp
and garbage, and my own horrid cry all

sounded like quiet voices next to me.
I thought no God would ever listen for a plea
lost in aimless whisper, so matter-of-fact
and weary. And that thought lingered
to sting the rawness over and over.

As in, just what good is a good cry?
Like the one Miss Minerva urged on me
in the old school cloakroom, huge and musty-
black as a cavern or cathedral. "Let it all
out," she cooed and left me with those sodden
coats, sour as sheep-stink and lined on hooks
like spooks or judges. If I'd been older or
able to un-sob myself, I would have wondered
if grim virginity worked in the practice
of her wisdom, or came as its pure result.
The bullies still slouched outside on
the corner, blue smoke billows frozen
above their heads. So the coach told me
to soak my mitts in salt, not my face
and that was the course I finally took.
A smack won't sting so badly when the skin
gets leathered up, but it will linger
to warm up a wet nerve down there,
just a little later. So that old scald
on my cheeks startled me when I lifted
the drunk old woman off the floor
of the midnight bus station. Booze
and urine leaking from her yellow fat
had soured her dress so much I went faint.
But her hot tears staining my chest, right
over the snapping gator on my shirt, must
have triggered my own stored salt. I was
retching though as I patted her back
saying "There" again and again, as if I'd
found a spot that echoed right. I might

have been the last person to hold her
in this world, but I don't think it mattered.
Nor did my own tears empty any hurt.
But I thought then that none of my thinking
and hearing was supposed to matter. All
I had to do was hold on and try not to vomit.

Riding the Lions

The sparrows, I'd forgotten them.
Almost tame, they hopped pecking
between the paws of the library
lions when I was a boy long
ago. Astraddle the smooth backs,
colder than I ever expected,
I dangled my legs above their
fussy flutter. The traffic's slam-
bangs and screeches couldn't drown
the murmur of their ceaseless cheeping.
My cousin rode the other
and it was grand to sit a minute
behind the enormous calm
of long stone faces so grave and noble
above the heads of people. A bum
fed them split corn and seeds
from somewhere and we thought
that's what bums did—fed birds
and loafed all day about the city,
murmuring and tittering to the air.
Because everything comes from some
thing, everyone from some one, some-
where, I'm sure sparrows still skitter
around sleepy yet living lions
in the Bronx Zoo or Zimbabwe.
But these are gone and the bum
my son and I saw today was crawling
through his own vomit up a snowbank
before The Museum of Natural History
and weeping. Somewhere,
it doesn't matter where anymore,

having a wrong idea became more
than being wrong. The older
cousin who hoisted us up there
is long dead and my youngest son
is already too old to climb on a lion
and I'm amazed that I remember.

Biloxi Beach

As his friends sauntered ahead, he stooped
to pluck a plastic gizmo from the tarry beach
scum roping the tidal edge. One of hundreds
of sun-yellow speckles tangled in brown kelp
and seaweed silage laid up on the littoral
slope in one tediously meandering hayrow.
While his fingers twiddled its snug tubes
and knobs, he thought "to inseminate lizards"
and felt a salt grain of regret to be left
alone with such bright wit. A whim tugged
in him to gather them. As he'd hoarded
sorted piles as a boy: clams by color,
scallops by size, a motley of spiral conches
like a plunder of strewn gems and doubloons
heaped in casual splendor around him.
Alone beyond all earshot, he'd cackled
and rasped in pirate Cockney to his loot,
gibbering to grinning bones, dribbling
handfuls on his head in an insane orgy
of absolutely happy avarice. But this gadget
held no mineral glitter or harmonious whorls.
Just litter in his hand. His clump of friends
was just a far-off wiggle of familiar colors.

He remembered a herd of yellow seahorses
marooned in full morning sun on a long ago
shore. Any way he poked their tails, curled
or straight, they shrank gaunt and stiff.
Their eyes shrivelled and sank away to nothing.
Just enormous sockets. He picked a sandpail
full before the stink sickened him.

He dumped them on the fly-blown mullet
gaping white-eyed behind the dunes
as if death stayed on as rotting agony.
That summer he grew bored with shells
and churned a paddle-boat beyond the life-
guard's hoarse threats to meet the sun
as it sank beneath the edge of the end
of the world. Lo and behold, another end
stretched just as far beyond. As it still did,
and with a small squeeze his stomach remembered,
and then forgot, how being lost once felt.
His plastic lizard-valve was as odd and lovely
as anything stinking from the sea,
and he churned through mushy sand to show it.

Vacationer

Mist rises and the cork twitches.
It's not a cork, but a red and white
plastic bobber molded and hand-glued
in Taiwan, of course. The old cork corks
came from Spain, got cut in balls
and drilled for the peg in Ohio.
Even the young still say "the cork."

Nonetheless, hills stacked in layers
behind the tranquil lake clear one after
another as the sun floats up. A kingfisher
swoops and squawks, a pair of dragonflies
twirl by in calm conjoinment. It seems
passions don't get too personal in nature,
which is nice for the first cup of coffee.
Whatever nibbles below is not too serious.
Nor is the vacationer who, without heat,
wonders for the first time in that day
if his house in the city has been ransacked.
And just what is insured? And for what?
A boat buzz down the lake's far haze ceases
and waves wash in, hush-hush, on the stones.

A styrofoam shred, whiter than a shiner
bobbing dead, nudges the cork that sits stolid
in mincing dips and crests. Such a brave
and cheerful little jig! On winking ripples
it bows and wheels like a stormtossed bark.
Or barque, as some still write. When it all
explodes this stuff will blow and float willy-

nilly. "Ubiquitous and immortal," Melville
described the whale long before plastic cork.
No one still says "Will I, nill I." The first
waterskier groans through the lake's center
like a buzzsaw. Though now it's called a skill-
saw. That's ridiculous, he thinks, a thing
must be alive in the first place to be immortal.

But he's still serene, this vacationer. Serene
as the hoariest Buddhists in Tibet. Though more
live in Hollywood or Bologna now. He watches
The bobber's stillness. Way up the lake's glare
A boat buzz starts. All things snarl and unsnarl,
he thinks, meaning tangle. It's the meaninglessness
of things. And from the cabin high up on the hill,

he hears the telephone's first cheerful jingle.

He Couldn't Know

he said, "and you still love him
just as much; don't fret what is.
We'll love only in each fierce moment."
After each one, she kept her wan face
to the wall and always her shoulders
shook for a little bit, but she came
back each week. He talked at the sun
freckles shaking there to soothe her
back into his arms, but his own words
got old questions smoldering in
his head. Like, is what is beautiful
loved because it's beautiful, and not
beautiful because it's loved? Or,
what do gods who don't exist love
and not love, and why can't they agree?
He couldn't know and in the quiet
while he smoked on the lightly
shaking bed these irksome words
kept swirling like the blue clouds
above his head. And at the end
of each day's moments, they stood
reflected in fifty motel windows
next to the sun glare blazing off
her hood as he talked hard and fast
like a conductor with his hands
and she held kleenex to her face.
Only a God should have seen shame
so naked. And each scene got worse
and he couldn't know if any one
of them was but a moment,
of the very essence, of their end—

78

so frenzied their love became in
those rooms scented like pine
and lemons. Such ardent moments,
arduous as swimming to the end
of the ocean, they each sank in an
oblivion so deep each other's wild
cries were faint as gull screams
on a horizon and the silence after
felt thick and airless as the death
of time. Then a denouement:
when she did not come or phone.
And he knew again from the pain
and gladness swirling in his chest,
like the sun and moon sometimes
wobble, glittering off the same
surface, that love is not at all
the same as loving. Though he knew
he couldn't know the difference.

The End of the World

—*for Michael Heffernan*

Funny how this topic comes up
or falls down at parties where
color che sanno of Art & Humanity
make with the *bel parlare.*
Like leaning on a railing in Hell
chatting with Dante and Virgil
when an enormousmonster suddenly
slimes right up in your faces
like those dolphins grinning
like mongoloids at Seaworld
and then subsides. Who of us
from the old world understands
this wine and cheese rage anyway—
brusquely spartan as office receptions
yet always held at dinner hour?

Even our pointy domes glow ruddy-hale
from sisyphean huffs and puffs on
jogging tracks and nautilus dreadnaughts.
And talk comes so easy now. We just
name facts and ideas with new names.
Not an actual dropping of names
but more like the small tossing up
in a tennis serve. So why follow through
when all points are made? But then,
PLUNK! The End of the World.

We—*genus irritabile vatum*—
lamented the Life of the Mind

pro and conning whether our pre-schoolers'
playstudy presented a correct Marxist
formula when the post-destructionist
who is usually such fun at parties
in his poloshirt/nehrujacket outfit
humming Bob Marley through an archaic
smile to signify a world cargo cult
said "Who cares?"

And in the hush as our minds scrambled
to name all Blame by genus and species
a pussycat stalked into the midst
of our lives and sank her claws
in the rug. Stretching in savage insolence
with her high-tailed ass in our faces
she roared without a sound and instantly
the red grease vienna sausages congealed
to a bloody paste. Such signs mean
everything and therefore nothing.
And then as always rises to fall
in the shrill silence of this topic
someone told the moral of a hermit/
ascetic who never changed despite
his fame and government grants
who said if he knew the world
would end tomorrow he'd just plant
another plum tree. And we all
nodded up and down as we always do
at wisdom. Neo-Panglossian Pragmatism
was the winning name and we chattered
home in our volkswagens. For without
skepticism and terrified of faith
we're strangely happy right here
at the End of the World.

Paratactic Prayer

"This sort of life is your passport into
the sky, to a union with those who have
finished their lives on earth...."
　　　—Cicero, *Somnium Scipionis*

Squinting too long into acrid urine
wafting off old vellum, I pause
to daub salty crust off lizard lids
with the corner of my cowl and raise
them naked to heaven. O Holy Ghost!
How long will my thoughts stay fixed
upon the earth? City lights blur
all but a few stars and a fat wad
of gray cloud obscures the moon
hovering full above my bed, hard
and thin. I face damp stone
listening to fretful wind hiss
in the chinks. Sin surrounds us.

Even pillows tight around my head
can't muffle the screeching tires
of the brutish fornicators who run
our town brawling home from bars,
banging metal to the jangled beat
of their beastlust. When the moon
swells ripe with wanton juices
what I yearn to hear, Lord,
is Your celestial music. *Reliqui
Caelites*, Cicero named stars
he gazed upon in sublime quiet.
They chopped off his hands, yanked
out his tongue and our *lingua* rots.

Because I believe stars loony-tune
our lives I'm no pagan or parlor-

snake sleazing up on the young wives
to say, "Say, what's your sign?"
as they bend so sweet and juicy
over the kohlrabi in the Supermarket.
This is no rhubarb: that poky old moon
soft-shoes between clouds growling
a Louis Armstrong bass, just as Cicero
said it did. Stars screech glass-
busting high as the fatlady sings
when goodguys die. I believe
Your Creed, O Hallowed Haunt: souls
are fiery gas—blue sparks pilot
deep in our rancid grease. Mongrels
that cuff moonbeams from their ears
and snap twinkles itching their tails
hear it and howl for respite
in city canyons. I wring my hands numb
with prayer. I feel the same sin
seep through me that moon-sucks the sea
in and out bringing bitches to heat.

I saw once a silver glint dart
beneath riffles to thrash scarlet
froth in the shallows. Chill iron
scalded my tongue tip. The same
savagery sparkles on the spiked ends
of their purple hair as they stagger
in the factory's weeded parkinglot.
I hear bottles smash against plywood
windows, prayers shrieked to Satan—
Pictish words for love and nightsoil.
The moon slices through shredded clouds
and yet, like a fixed thought in
a seething mind, hovers forever still.
Oh why do You love them so? Send one
small sign to me, Your true servant—
stammering monk of most bitter gall!
O Smite them, God, thigh and bone!

Timor Mortis: Sermo

"Who're you," my student asked, "to tell me what's
so?" A challenge, and in the stomach-taut
silence, I realized those holes in the famous
classroom walls, where wise Nabokov once taught,
had been punched by fists. Flustered by the flank
attack, my mind fumbled for credentials instead
of wisdom. A sour redolence I'd always thought
was chalk, spilled soda pop and pubescent sweat
was also sullen fear, gone angry there. Of what?
The ceiling dripped ooblek globs. It oozed
off walls and crept between their German sneakers.
Whatever from, I caught it too. And the gray wind

felt cruel, but fresh at least, when I stepped out.
The campus hill fell so steeply I half-stumbled
to Stewart Ave., still brick-paved with trolley
grooves, where I trudged through thicket to hop
the gully into Ithaca's first city graveyard.
"Boneyard Cut," Cornell's first students called
that half-mile meander between a quiet bristle
of mossy headstones to the flats. No cars then,
they bounded down to their evening beer
and moaned back up at the slate sky each morning
on the long march up to wisdom. I squinted
one eye into a streak of stinging ice-snits.

Peppered by a fast slant of sharp crystals,
I finally ducked behind an obelisk. A six-foot
granite needle up-thrusting from a veined,
marble ball. What's it called—"cultural residue?"
Hoo-doo of Osiris, in this case. A local copy
of clutter the Corsican thug hauled home

84

to out-do Alexander, our "primal" juvenile
delinquent. Maybe that student-brat was right;
all I seemed to know was the frivolous history
of pointed ornaments. I remembered this awesome
pricker from when I was an under-aged sneak.
Crouching in the smelly shadow of its shaft,

I'd mooncalfed to a wine bottle, murmuring
erotic laments to the dead. The gray kleenex wad
I now fished out to mop my running nose and eyes
looked like a miniature mummy. Soak it good,
I thought, and like my brain it'll bloom to
resurrect last season's salty snot from musty
lint. And my old heart with its same slow leak;
I'd lugged it back to that same sorrow spot, too.
I'm sure I looked like a caricature of last
century's tomb-pose, snuffling and wiping
myself next to a droop of small hemlock where
the wind's whine tried to match my weather.

But I was too mean for grief—glad the day
blew so filthy it cleared my path of joggers.
Every American, but me. Only one huffed by,
panting righteous steam and damp as a Spanish
flagellant sweating sin, wringing out cholesterol
poisons. Her gaze was as vacant-blank as a Greek
statue's, but her lovely ass pumped quite nicely.
So serious though—she'd have to talk about it,
before and after, as if it was a French movie
so resonant with meaningful silences you could
talk about smelling the colors. So I didn't look
at her with heat. I gritted my teeth and hunched,

thinking joggers are like snowmobiles that intrude
on deep and quiet places the way ambition crowds
a calm mind into anger. As sleet smeared the air
she'd jostled through, I wondered what had become

of pondering—a slow heft of thought like a path
looping the long way round for points of view.
As in churchyards, twilight, cowbells (but faint),
and a couple owls hooting the moon from a busted
    belfry.
I imagined the student-boy's blank eyes glancing
at the rigid numbers winking on his wrist if I tried
to tender such fancy poetic connotation in his class.
He'd paid to learn the technics, how to rig up

effects both plain and special into linear formulae,
tried and true. He'd already gotten high school credit
in Pragmatic Caring and Small Attitude Repair. Feelings
courses. He was ready for Equipment. A "real world"
glowed on the horizon and he heard its hum, vicious
and thrilling like the sound of shadows writhing
into substance off the walls, or out of those holes.
So much, so fast—there's only time to breathe deeply
and empty the mind before every lesson. If the eye
lingered on slough and scale, a stiff curl at the lichen's
edge, then the breath couldn't pace an efficient rhythm.
And if he should pause on any path in those woods,

he might see that over half of everything is rotting.
And that's depressing. Gloom like that could lead
to ponderous thought. Sneering, I conjured up
the boy among the rows of cold stones, to pretend
to give him what he wanted. Suppose, I proposed,
we hollywood this boneyard hill? Bright day
gets black as a bad bruise; sky and earth grumble
into a roar—it's all done with a moog and lenses.
Cheap and vivid, see? The hill cracks open wide
to horn music, hummocks erupt, spiked with foul
bones waving ragged pennants from rotted shrouds.
Pan across gaping graves, jaws and sockets

to zoom sharply back from the jelly-blank eye

of the town's best-loved virgin, until she's fully
splayed on a dirt heap in stinking technicolor.
Flashback to her laid out lily-lovely, white dress
in a ring of black mourners. Then back to it crushed
above her hips, and to get the rating, let her blue
vulva beckon for a full second between a spread of
     bloat.
Cut-frame fast to her other lips, shrunk in wanton grin
and then—holograph her right up out of her corpse.
I imagined my transparent student nodding at me,
eager mouth agape. Now there's some real symbols!
Sam Clemens mocked that script one hundred years
     ago,

but it still sells. In fact, the kid probably
picked up his "thing" for sleek technique in a symbol
seminar on the famous ether hill. Each version's
gimmick was frozen on white in the black droning
     room
as if wisdom had been caught in the act of happening.
Dripping from my eyes, nose, and maybe heart
in wind gone sour, I couldn't think of one fact
of knowledge that always worked. What had I
to offer the young? For that's the name for courses
now—offerings, raw meat always fresh for angry gods.
No wonder they're all the time afraid and running,
I pondered. For I'd set out down that path again.

Rigorous training, I thought, that's what I'll teach:
hard drill instead of strategy. But Horace meant
patient labor walks arm-in-arm with the angelic mind
and luck, always luck. One alone is for empty yearning.
"Suppose," the old grouch crowed, "some pothead
painted a horse's face on a beauty queen
and tailed her off in a fish's hideous slime?
Silly, no?" We think Horace is silly now because
we still purse our lips, like so, and squint

into Pablo's pictures as if to blur helped focus.
We pull our goatbeards, real or imagined,
with our thumbs and pointers and of course we nod—

the nod of fashion. For there's a *passegiato* nod,
a jogger's nod paced fast within the exhale,
a nod of heroin, a papal nod and so many more
in a whole catalogue of nods. I couldn't keep up
with all the costumes. Though it seems like the same
teenager from Los Angeles is under every Mao cap
or pinstripe. I taught my dog, Luca, to sit
and wait until I nod. She loves to squirm her neck
and back on any ripe flyblown meat and her spots
are always in fashion. Those yellow sprinkles,
offerings at the gravestone's corners recalled
a picture of her: burrowing to the warm core

of the compost to snort the wisping ghosts of steam
when she got there. Luca owns the purest frivolity.
Churning that steady spume of rotten flocculence
behind her, she was efficient to no purpose and more
at peace with herself than any jogger or yoga pupil
can get. My daughter was chirping a TV theme once
as we walked some woods on fire with death, "Fame,
I wanna live forever." I pointed where Luca
squatted to squeeze out a fresh pile, proud steam
and glisten. "Horace," I intoned, "says we're
destined to die, and all our works as well." "Gross,"
she said, "that's really gross." And I was pleased

she got my point. For I was a teacher, though all
my churning knowledge seemed to cascade down
in fissures, to gurgle out of sight in darkness.
Pondering like that, I'd ambled in the lessening
storm to where the rich people's old mausoleums
are built into the hillside. Where our moans' echos
down the air vents used to scare the drunks and lovers

years ago. I paused to give my invisible student
another lesson. I was sure, wherever he really was,
he was picking his nose over a psychology
paperback. I didn't switch him on to buzz and waver
like a laser-picture, but *summoned* him as Coleridge

or Edgar Poe might have. Read Poe, I instructed him,
clear as cellophane and still nodding. Read Poe;
his brain was heavy as an angel's. Poe would know
what it meant when the pepsi-ad/child-star
floated between bursting green and crimson bombs
with his head on fire. Read Edgar Allan Poe!
And drop that shuck course, Death & Dying.
No matter how many easy credits it offers,
it's still a lie when the sychophants of Doctor
Sickman Fraud say you can't imagine your own death.
What were the dark-age Irish monks doing as they
nodded down to sleep in their own rude coffins?

Subliminally denying? What? Isn't it always screwing?
Deconstruct the Fear of God and it's just another
horny itch. We must assume they lusted for that fun-
      fear,
the rollercoaster dip in the bad-clam stink of sex.
Phrase that in airless latinates and their shivering
passion will be safe for graduate study. My special
effect was failing. My student, no longer nodding,
grew faint in a shy glimmer of sunlight and faded
against a vault's facade. Why did my absurd lecture
voice always get so urgent? Why did I always testify,
instead of really teaching? Why not do racquet ball
therapy like everyone else? Ashamed now, I let

the boy evaporate into the tomb's red sandstone.
I understood and despised his impatience, real or
imagined, with such a muskrat ramble through the
      jumble.

One of those rough-hewn pediments and cast-iron gates
reminded me of Old Walt Flowerbeard's tomb
in Camden. He got his sentimental pals to shell out
for a death cottage, while he yawped it up on Lincoln
Tours. My lip curled, thinking of his famous chant,
"Myself, Death, Myself, Death," warbled to a juicy
moonlit lap of Coney Island wavelets. Emerson's
Handbook for American Bullies in one fat paw,
the other thrilling up delicious bumps over yards

of baby-soft flesh, he did his hoary mantra to summon
back the hot fondles of streetcar hoodlums.
What a jerk! But he wasn't shamed to be the fool
he was and with sleepy eyes he roared through his life.
He screwed his heart wide open to gush so it over-
tuned his brain—the brain he'd wanted in his tomb,
that got dropped on the autopsy floor instead.
He wrote he'd come back to feel us up when we
    pondered
on him, and I was ashamed the thought got me moving
on. And my squeamishness reminded me of his logical
opposite, Sallow Emily who entombed herself from
    touch
to keep house all her days, all in white, for Daddy—

Thanatos, preacher-judge who spanked her oh-so
soundly with his glance. It was so easy to nod
in leering seen-it-all contempt for her hymnal drone:
Amazing Grace freeze-dried to the deathwatch buzz
of a maggot-heavy fly. Her horny itch was analyzed.
But she'd also walked through some kind of hell
with her head on fire. Her God-fear wasn't the same
kind of shame I was starting to scratch. I thought
her knowledge might've been the beginning of wisdom,
and maybe holy. My anger had felt righteous,
but standing at the bottom of all those bones,
it came to me that fear is a father of anger

90

and fear of death mothers all fears. At University Ave.,
I jumped off the stone wall onto those Ithaca streets
I used to dawdle on after school. I remembered how
    soon
the light failed for evening, how Victorian cornices
glowered on my heart's horny ache, the same slow
    leak.
The same houses lined up, but lo-and-behold latexed
in bold, happy chromotints. In my own long-ago days,
the sky glared white on a sunny afternoon and grass
shone like a bin of new shiny nails. I was wrong,
of course, but I thought no one truly sad could live
in houses blushing and blooming such vivid hues.
And often truly, no one did. The college grad wood-

worker who box-sawed out the professional signs
probably sold retail from an Edwardian manse himself.
On the new mall, old features in strange faces, all
tanned from jogging, struck me. Everyone I loved
was once the color of cold oatmeal. I think I saw
the school bully in his lawyer suit speaking kindly
to the idiot boy who used to weep and drool and soil
himself in a corner of the bus station. Everywhere
I looked there was nobody to pity but myself.
Starting in rage, I'd pondered and lectured my way
down through the dead, expecting my town to have
    kept
like a museum its old grime and smells of sorrow.

Like in the old black and white movie, trucks had come
one night loaded with pods the size of small kayaks.
Next morning folks were the same, just the same, but
    so
flawlessly perfect, so perfectly themselves, they were
unbearable. We want only our angels perfect.
Where was my pod, I wondered? And I guess my pose
was wistful—Chaplinesque, let's say. I felt so short

91

and baggy with my head beginning a fever, cocked up
at the gothic turrets on the old brick high school.
They'd "converted" it, as if from some unspeakably
cruel religion, into hip boutiques offering tofu
and handmade dulcimers. How'd I miss the grand
recycle? When everyone unsheathed like new limas,
instead of slimy and squalling for another spank?
Through my old homeroom window, I saw a fuzzy face
in wire-rims munching the moral vegetables of health
and probably from exhaustion tears started bulging
my pouches a bit. It sure as hell wasn't nostalgia.
There'd been a teacher there whose hand was maimed
in the shape of a vicious claw which he dug deep
into the necks of smaller boys. It was a famous joke,
a school tradition. And it was there I was first
tracked "dull normal" and after the second-string
wrestlers got enough of the echo, like cymbals

crashing, that made them happy from heaving my head
into the lockers, it felt like I was trying to breathe
greasy shadows. It was an awful place, but it was my
awful place and I learned there it is not "OK"
to blubber like a wimp on the public street.
So in my desperation not to bawl, I decided
it was "OK" for the weirdy-beard to chomp rotten
bean sprouts in my old homeroom. That was easy.
And so I forgave him for loving all of personkind
and the critters and for always questioning authority
on my behalf and for looking like a koala bear.
And I heard my student's voice and since his whine

was exactly mine, I had to forgive him too.
"Whoso loveth instruction loveth knowledge:
but he that hateth reproof *is* brutish."
It hadn't been my day to teach; I was no teacher,
but much better. I was a witness sent down through
the dead to testify like those called before me

from their shops and fields, summoned to sing
by fire lit in their heads. Down the sidewalk to me
wobbled our town's oldest upright man, his hair
a pure cottonball of white fire. He put each foot
down so carefully, letting the earth's firmness rise up
in each leg, before the next step. And as a baby's

smooth face can be wise and ancient, his wrinkles
were soft as an infant's. He was doing the old people's
exercises, rolling his arms slowly, in grand circles
the way large birds prepare to rise or land.
He wasn't an angel, but he seemed to be practicing.
He was just being alive that day and I felt
like crying all over again. It had been a harsh day
and he was the first one I'd come to love. *Timor
mortis*, only a fool would keep lighting matches
in the face of conflagration. I would forgive myself
every morning and God at night. Then all you other
bastards, I'd forgive you too—even if it was just one

a year and I had to live forever to get there.

March 1984, Ithaca, New York

About the Author

Looking into the Heart of Light is William Hathaway's fifth book of poems. He came of age in Ithaca, New York, and currently lives in the woods on the side of a mountain above Porter Corners, New York. In the intervening years between his childhood and his forty-third year, he lived in Europe, Massachusetts, Montana, Iowa, and Louisiana. He has supported himself primarily as a teacher of writing and literature. Since he grew up in an academic family, his essays and short stories reflect a heartfelt interest in higher education, though he is currently an untenured visitor in those halls. His three children have pretty much grown and flown, but when Hathaway sits down to eat a sandwich and recite poetry to his deaf dalmatian, that dog looks up to him with such passionate concentration that all the years of obscure toil are bathed and salved in golden light....

[*Editor's note:* Mr. Hathaway, who wrote the above paragraph, is presently a visiting associate professor at Union College, Schenectady. He was a Bread Loaf Fellow in 1983, and his work appears in three recent anthologies.]